INTERPERSONAL PSYCHOTHERAPY
FOR PERINATAL DEPRESSION:
A GUIDE FOR TREATMENT DURING PREGNANCY AND THE POSTPARTUM PERIOD

(IPT-P)

Margaret G. Spinelli, MD

DEDICATED TO
DRS MYRNA WEISSMAN AND GERALD KLERMAN
FOR THEIR OUTSTANDING WORK IN THE FIELDS OF
PSYCHOTHERAPY, PSYCHIATRY AND PSYCHOLOGY

PERINATAL DEPRESSION

The fact that the prevalence of depression during pregnancy is 11.0% in the first trimester and 8.5% in the second and third trimester dispels the myth of unconditional well-being during gestation.[1] After delivery, prevalence of major and minor depression begins to rise and is highest in the third month at 12.9%. Higher rates have been reported in minority women and women with low socioeconomic status.[2] In a study of impoverished inner-city single women depression rates were 27.5% and 24.5 % at two intervals during pregnancy. Investigators have also found that 47 % of women of low SES and 20% of women with higher SES scored >10 on the Beck Depression Inventory (BDI).[2,3]

Depression during pregnancy can have detrimental consequences for women, children, and the family unit. Women with a history of depression are particularly vulnerable to pregnancy-associated recurrence. Risk factors for depression during pregnancy [4-9] include personal or family history of mood disorder; stressors such as marital dysfunction and demographic variables such as young age, minimal education, increased number of children and a history of child abuse. Chronic stressors, financial and housing problems, negative life events, alcohol abuse and inadequate social supports are all linked to increased depressive symptomatology during pregnancy.

Timely and appropriate treatment is vital in order to avoid negative health related behaviors such as poor nutrition and weight loss. Pregnant depressed women are more vulnerable to nicotine, drug and alcohol abuse and failure to obtain adequate prenatal care,[10] all factors which compromise fetal development. Maternal stress and depression during pregnancy are associated with lower birth weight and gestational age, deliveries by Caesarean section, newborn irritability and infants admitted to the neonatal care unit. [11,12]

Adverse outcomes of depression during pregnancy also include, pre-eclampsia, low birth weight, preterm delivery, post-partum depression, and suicide.[13-21] Neurobehavioral effects of infants of depressed mothers have been reflected in frontal lobe activity on EEG. [22] Prenatal maternal depression has been found to alter amygdala functional connectivity in 6-month-old infants.[23] A recent analysis from the Centers for Disease Control and Prevention's surveillance system from 17 states over 4 years found 94 pregnancy-related suicides and 139 homicides from 2003 to 2007.[24,25] Half of these violent deaths were associated with intimate partner violence and psychiatric illness, which are common in pregnancy-associated suicide.

The evidence that psychosocial stressors and negative life events are precipitants to antepartum depression suggests that a behavioral treatment like Interpersonal Psychotherapy for Perinatal Depression (IPT-P) is beneficial, particularly in women with difficult life circumstances.[26] During the course of IPT-P, maternal-fetal attachment may be explored during gestation in order to facilitate resolution of conflicts or ambivalence before delivery.

The fact that one half of pregnant depressed women will have a postpartum depression (PPD) emphasizes the importance of prevention and early identification of risk factors.[1] Although the DSM5 suggests that postpartum depression should be diagnosed in the first 4 postpartum weeks, most clinicians and researchers use six months or one year postpartum as the cutoff time for diagnosis. The combined period prevalence shows that as many as 19.2% (7.1%) of women have a depressive episode (major depressive episode) during the first 3 months postpartum.[1, 2] Marital discord is a frequent outcome of postpartum depression. Suicide is one of the leading causes of perinatal maternal mortality. Very few studies have focused on suicide attempts in the perinatal period. Special attention to suicide risk is particularly necessary during pregnancy for women with severe mental illness and a history of alcohol abuse in the perinatal period.[13]

Childhood abuse, intimate partner violence, maternal low educational attainment, low socioeconomic status, poor social support, and history of mental illness have all been consistently identified as risk factors for post-partum depression in low-income and middle-income countries.[20]

Infants of depressed postpartum mothers appear to have deficits in postnatal growth. They are more likely to have low scores on the Bayley Scales of Infant Development and more likely to have fewer cognitive, motor, orientation or engagement skills. Furthermore, child behavior problems, and delayed language development in infants at 12 months of age are also associated with PPD.[27, 28]

Demonstrating the importance of early identification of maternal depression, the US Preventive Services Task Force (USPSTF) has published a clinically influential report recommending screening of US pregnant and post-partum women for depression. These recommendations went into effect in 2016 [29] throughout the United States for early identification, treatment and prevention of perinatal depression.

INTERPERSONAL PSYCHOTHERAPY

Recommendations for treatment of antepartum depression by the American Psychiatric Association (APA) and the American College of Obstetrics and Gynecology (ACOG) include the use of psychotherapy for mild-to-moderate depression.[30, 31] Pregnancy is the paramount time for identification, treatment and prevention because depression in pregnancy is the strongest predictor of PPD. Treating antenatal and postnatal depression has the potential for far-reaching effects such as maintaining the well being of the maternal-fetal environment, preventing PPD, promoting maternal infant attachment and preventing infant and family morbidity. Parturient women are one of the most available populations to antenatal, postnatal and pediatric clinics and clinicians. Yet, we frequently miss the opportunity for identification, intervention and prevention. IPT has been adapted to perinatal depression (IPT-P) [26] using Klerman and Weissman's model and manual of IPT.[32]

In 1984, Gerald Klerman, Myrna Weissman et al. published *Interpersonal Psychotherapy of Depression* the original IPT manual, [32] which should be the first manual read for the new student of IPT. While parts of this manual use and reference the original Klerman and Weissman manual, this adaptation is specific for depression during pregnancy. Klerman and Weissman's guidelines remain the same.

IPT was adapted from the school of interpersonal psychiatry based on the theories of Harry Stack Sullivan.[33] Sullivan emphasized the importance of social roles as they relate to family, friends and community. Another figure that embraced this school of thought, Adolf Meyer[34] of John's Hopkins Medical School viewed mental illness as an attempt by the individual to adapt to one's environment. Klerman and Weissman et al applied these theories to a brief psychotherapy treatment for depression.

In 1984 Klerman, Weissman and colleagues developed interpersonal psychotherapy for depression.[32] It was designed to address symptoms of depression and subsequent interpersonal conflicts. While interpersonal issues may not cause depression, they frequently occur in the context of depression. The focus of treatment is depression as a biological illness.[32] IPT is a 12-16 week treatment with a fixed endpoint created to treat nonpsychotic major depression.[32] The goals of IPT include decreased symptoms of depression and resolution of interpersonal conflicts. Although emphasis is on the present, treatment may utilize the past as it relates to the present.

The interpersonal psychotherapist begins evaluation and treatment using the following data: [32]
1. Inventory of the patient's current and past relationships
2. Pattern of relationships as they endure over time
3. Beliefs, expectations and role changes
4. Associated affect and interpersonal experience

In contrast to IPT, psychodynamic psychotherapy is commonly a long- term treatment that emphasizes the role of the unconscious defenses and transference. It explores early conflicts as manifested in the present.[32.] The aim of the treatment is interpretation and resolution of the transference.

Similar to IPT, cognitive behavioral therapy (CBT) is a brief therapy designed to treat depression. It is based on the theory that thoughts and behavior determine feelings, i.e. that negative thoughts promote feelings of depression. CBT utilizes therapist assigned tasks and homework assignments for the patient.[32]

In the NIMH Treatment of Depression Collaborative Research Program, [35] IPT was shown to significantly reduce depressive symptoms and improve function. In our work with antepartum depression, supervision of psychotherapy using videotapes of IPT-P therapy sessions were conducted in accordance with methods used in the NIMH Collaborative Study. [35]

EFFICACY OF IPT IN THE PERINATAL POPULATION

Several clinical trials have demonstrated the efficacy of IPT in the treatment of major depression, perinatal depression[36] depressed adolescents[37] and maintenance treatment[38] of major depression. Furthermore, there is increased scientific evidence of the benefits of psychotherapy for depressed subjects treated with IPT compared to controls is associated with brain and physiological changes.[39] In a comprehensive meta-analysis, [40] Cuijpers et al reviewed ninety studies, which included 11,434 participants. The authors found that IPT is effective in the acute treatment of depression and may be effective in the prevention of new depressive disorders and in preventing relapse.

IPT is a noninvasive treatment of proven efficacy that is available to this underserved population. IPT-P has been a central theme for treatment in the perinatal period, a time when some women wish like to avoid medication because of pregnancy or breastfeeding. O'Hara and Stuart[41] were the first to develop and test IPT in the postpartum population and found that IPT is an efficacious treatment for postpartum depression that reduced depressive symptoms and improved social adjustment.

Spinelli et al[26, 42,43] developed a model of IPT for depression during pregnancy. We conducted three research studies, which demonstrated efficacy of IPT-P for pregnant depressed women. Our first trial included a preponderance of Latina patients from our catchment area at Columbia demonstrating its efficacy in a Hispanic, immigrant, and Spanish speaking population. In the last trial 479 prospective research participants were referred from the obstetrics departments of New York Presbyterian Hospital at Columbia University College of Physicians and Surgeons (Columbia), New York Presbyterian Hospital at Weill Cornell Medical College (Cornell), and St Luke's Roosevelt Hospital (all located in New York, New York). We conducted a 3-site controlled bilingual (Spanish and English) treatment trial from September 2005 to May 2011. We compared the efficacy of interpersonal psychotherapy for antepartum depression to a parenting education program control for women who met Diagnostic and Statistical Manual of Mental Disorders (DSM-IV) criteria for major depressive disorder. Our final analysis including women with moderate depression at baseline found that IPT-P was more effective than parenting education for depression during pregnancy.[43]

Klier et al[44] adapted an IPT group model for the treatment of postpartum depression and found that depression scores decreased significantly from pre- to post-treatment up to 6 months. Zlotnick et al[45] had equal success in a pilot study of an interpersonal-therapy-oriented group intervention in women receiving public assistance and Brandon et al's[46] unique clinical trial contribution demonstrated success in Partner-Assisted Interpersonal Psychotherapy for perinatal depression.

Grote et al,[47] in a culturally relevant adaptation of IPT demonstrated that IPT ameliorates depression during pregnancy, prevents depressive relapse and improves social functioning up to six months postpartum. Grote et al[48] also evaluated a culturally relevant, collaborative care intervention, (MOMCare), which included brief interpersonal psychotherapy. MOMCare showed significant improvement in quality of care, depression severity, and remission rates from before birth to 18 months post baseline for socioeconomically disadvantaged women. In a further study by Grote et al[49] collaborative depression care that included IPT had a greater impact on perinatal depressive outcomes for socioeconomically disadvantaged women with comorbid PTSD than for those without PTSD. Findings suggest that a stepped care treatment model, including IPT for high-risk pregnant women with both MDD and PTSD could be integrated into the services of a county public health system in the United States. Bhat et al.[50] found that IPT mitigated the risk of postpartum depressive symptoms and impaired functioning among women of low socioeconomic status who had antenatal depression and who experienced adverse birth events. Another unique pilot, [51] exploratory report on dyadic interpersonal psychotherapy for perinatal depression with postpartum dyadic psychotherapy focused on emotional development in the context of the mother-infant relationship. Two pilot studies found interpersonal psychotherapy effective in pregnant adolescents.[52]

A recent two-generation study by Schwartz et al[53] demonstrated that treating maternal depression benefits school-age children, especially in very high-risk families in which both mothers and children concurrently meet syndromal criteria for psychiatric disorders. Symptom remission was associated with improvement in child functioning. A small number reported clinically significant improvements out to 12 months postpartum.

Munieti[54] identified 11 clinical primary trials assessing the efficacy of IPT for postpartum depression, including 3 trials with group interventions (G-IPT) and one that required the presence of the partner (PA-IPT). They also identified six studies of interpersonal-psychotherapy-oriented preventive interventions for use in pregnancy. IPT studies showed overall clinical improvement in the most commonly used depression measures in postpartum depressed women and often-full recovery in several cases of treated patients. Evidence from clinical trials indicates that, when administered in monotherapy (or in combination with antidepressants), IPT may shorten the time to recovery from postpartum depression and prolong the time spent in clinical remission.

Interpersonal Psychotherapy for Perinatal Depression (IPT-P) is a time-limited treatment that focuses on a particular problem in the patient's life and relationships. The patient and therapist agree on the focus in the early sessions of therapy. It remains the central theme throughout the treatment. Because of the unique and developmental problems associated with gestation, an additional problem area addresses issues unique to pregnancy, which cannot be addressed using only the Klerman's original IPT problem set;[32] *grief, interpersonal role dispute, role transition and interpersonal deficits.* This fifth broad area, *complicated pregnancy* addresses problems specific to gestation such as undesired pregnancy, medical problems associated with pregnancy itself, obstetrical complications, multiple births and congenital anomalies.

Since pharmacological treatments may have unlikely adverse effects on the fetus, a risk/benefit analysis is the most appropriate method for intervention.[31] The most recent literature should be discussed with the patient so that she can make an informed decision. Although several clinical trials on the use of antidepressants have been performed, birth defects research is often unreliable because of retrospective data and poor methodology. Selected birth defects often differ from study to study, and findings are seldom replicated. Additional problems include insufficient power, confounders such as alcoholism, OTC drug use, other medication, illicit drug use, smoking or depression itself. The clinician must determine if the risk of using a medication outweighs the risk of the mother's illness. While IPT-P is an effective treatment, which precludes any possible danger to the fetus it is effective for mild to moderate depression. In an effort to establish guidelines for treating perinatal depression, this manual describes IPT-P as a principal method of delivering care, and a first line measure in the hierarchy of treatment guidelines.

PERINATAL PERIOD

Childbirth is a complicated experience.[55] Social situation; status and relationships are all subject to change. The pregnant woman begins to anticipate a progression from independence to a lifetime of responsibility. There is a transition in her role and a re-evaluation of her relationship with her own mother. Complicating the whole process, she must also prepare to separate from her child. While the importance of the rewarding, fulfilling aspects of motherhood once stressed and confirmed the female identity, we recognize now that some pregnant women may, in fact, have ambivalent or even hostile feelings towards the pregnancy and fetus.

While the journey from non-motherhood to motherhood is essentially the same for all, each woman approaches it through her own perceptions and her own social and psychological experiences. Pregnancy has been described as a period of emotional crisis.[56] In fact; it is addressed more appropriately as a developmental period in which the mother-to-be transitions from independence to motherhood. This process may stir feelings about other relationships or other losses.[57] The woman has increased dependency needs, and paradoxically fears both the loss of her identity as well as impending separation from the infant. If the woman has a history of complications such as stillbirth or spontaneous abortion, she may fear loss of the infant by death or illness.

The unique hormonal environment of pregnancy and childbirth has significant physiological and psychological sequelae. Pregnant and postpartum women experience a range of emotions from elation to fear to ambivalence. In addition, the woman must adjust to her own altered body image as well as the reactions of those around her.

The postpartum period is also a stressful time even for mothers who are not depressed. Depression in the postpartum period is complicated by disappointment because of the unexpected outcome and frequently experienced detachment from their infants. These mothers fail to experience the joy of early mothering. They may be unable to bond or care for their infant. Frequently they may find breastfeeding more difficult and frustrating. They are anxious, unable to sleep when the baby sleeps and feel guilty because they believe that they are failures ("bad mothers").

HIGH RISK PREGNANCY

Normal pregnancy results in the recognition of conflicts. The developmental and psychological tasks of the woman with a medically complicated pregnancy are cumbersome. Women with psychosocial stressors, poor support systems and lower SES have a more difficult time with the transition to motherhood. A high-risk pregnancy may result from complications, which include maternal disorders, obstetric difficulties or fetal compromise. These complications may contribute to an already existing anxiety and make this an even more stressful time.[58]

Maternal complications are usually pre-existing disorders which include hypertension, diabetes, cardiovascular disease, renal disease, positive HIV serology and malignancies. Obstetric factors include cervical incompetence, habitual abortions, preeclampsia, multiple gestation, placenta praevia and abruptio placenta. Other disorders that may create fetal compromise include uterine dysfunction, pelvic disproportion, and abnormal presentation, size or development of the fetus necessitating Cesarean section. Other fetal complications include intrauterine growth retardation and fetal distress. Any of the conditions may affect the outcome of the pregnancy and the life of the mother and infant. The medical risk and associated concerns may increase anxiety and guilt and precipitate depression.

DEPRESSION DURING PREGNANCY AND THE POSTPARTUM PERIOD

That women are protected from depression during pregnancy is a myth perpetuated in the literature. Social expectations are that a gravid woman's mood improves, or may even be elated during pregnancy. The stigma of mental illness is more prominent at this well-defined time in a woman's life. Emphasis on puerperal depression has focused on the postpartum period. Many postpartum depressed women recall the onset of depressive symptoms during pregnancy. The somatic complaints, which accompany pregnancy, are similar to the symptoms of depression, and often attributed to the pregnancy itself.[59] Complaints of fatigue, anergia, hypersomnia, appetite change and mood lability often challenge the clinician's differential diagnosis.

In my practice I like to discuss depression affecting three states: emotional, physical and cognitive. The reason is that cognitive impairments or physical symptoms may be more prominent and bothersome than mood changes. The pregnant woman may not recognize that her mood is depressed.

I explain these changes in the following way:
Emotional: depression, anxiety, irritability, anger, and crying and suicidal thoughts
Physical: psychomotor retardation, fatigue, decreased motivation, increased or decreased appetite, weight or sleep, slow speech
Cognitive: poor memory and concentration, low self-esteem, guilt, hopelessness

Depression during and after pregnancy is often associated with somatic complaints,[59] that may mimic the discomforts of the perinatal period. It is important for the clinician to determine whether or not the somatic symptoms of depression are attributable to pregnancy, stress or other associated factors. Klein and Essex[59] reviewed common complaints of pregnancy that may overlap with depressive symptoms such as fatigue, emotional lability, food cravings or aversions, nausea and vomiting, insomnia, diminished interest in sex and feeling overweight. Similarly, postpartum discomforts may also mimic depression. Postpartum depression has components of anxiety, fatigue, inability to sleep when the baby sleeps and problems with concentration. Standardized instruments, such as the Edinburgh Postnatal Depression Scale[60] have effectively determined the presence of depressive symptoms during pregnancy and after childbirth without emphasizing associated somatic concerns.

The symptoms of depression are often confusing to the woman herself. If unfamiliar with these well-defined symptoms,[59] the patient often attributes her mood to external stressors or discomforts of the perinatal period. Often related to depressive symptoms are the degree of stress and coping,[32] available social supports, absence of intimacy, marital conflicts, communication problems, marital separation, adjustment and transitions in work, family and community.

Antepartum depression may precipitate postpartum depression, which places the family at risk, and frequently impairs mother-infant interaction. IPT-P may prevent impaired attachment. Depressed postpartum women are at increased risk of having infants who are withdrawn, irritable, and who are difficult to console.[10] Children of depressed mothers have significant behavioral problems such as sleep and eating disorders, temper tantrums and delayed language development. Early development is marked by insecure attachment behavior secondary to mother's unresponsiveness to infant cues, and a lack of warmth and acceptance. Preschool effects include poor compliance and poor creativity in problem solving, anger and negativistic actions, intellectual deficits, impaired social function, school problems, poor attention skills, and a predisposition to depression itself. [61-64]

Weissman et al[65] demonstrated that depressed mothers' remission was associated with improved parenting and improvement in their child's mood. The high rate of depression among children of depressed mothers is well known. Weissman et al recruited 76 depressed mothers who entered into a medication clinical trial for depression and 135 of their eligible offspring ages 7-17 years. The mothers and children were assessed at baseline and periodically over 9 months by independent teams to understand the relationship between changes in children's symptoms and functioning and maternal remission or relapse. Maternal remission was associated with a decrease in the child's depressive symptoms. The mother's subsequent relapse was associated with an increase in the child's symptoms over 9 months. The effect of maternal remission on the child's improvement was partially explained by an improvement in the mother's parenting, particularly the change in the mother's ability to listen and talk to her child, but also reflected in her improvement in parental bonding. These findings could not be explained by the child's treatment. The group concluded that depressed mother's remission is associated with her improvement in parenting and a decrease in her child's symptoms. Her relapse is associated with an increase in her child's symptoms. Other serious sequelae of maternal mental illness are increased rates of accidental injury, child abuse and neglect.[64]

During the initial clinical evaluation, the clinician must determine the severity of depression in order to recommend the appropriate treatment. This is facilitated by the use of objective mood scales in order to determine if the depression is mild, moderate or severe. IPT-P is recommended for mild or moderate mood symptoms. Severe depression may need pharmacological intervention. In addition, I recommend using a mood scale every week to measure symptom resolution over the course of treatment. The question of whether or not somatic symptoms are valid indicators of depression in pregnant women suggests exclusion when assessing pregnant women for depression. The Edinburgh Depression Rating Scale (EPDS) is the gold standard scale for measuring symptoms during pregnancy because it does not have a somatic component.[60]

Rating scales with somatic symptoms like the Hamilton Rating Scale for Depression (HDRS-17)[66] should be used with caution when assessing perinatal depression because many depressive symptoms may mimic the discomforts of pregnancy and the postpartum period. To address this problem in our research study, we asked subjects whether or not a particular symptom was attributed to pregnancy (not scored) or to depression (endorse symptom). Our post hoc analysis revealed no differences between HDRS scores between groups when somatic symptoms were excluded[39] suggesting that the presence of these factors did not elevate their scores and that women tend to incorporate their own opinions about the etiology of symptoms.

Because there are no observer-rated scales that do not include somatic symptoms, the HDRS-17 is an important complement to self-report measures such as the EPDS. Both scales have excellent diagnostic validity, sensitivity and specificity. Both are highly predictive of major depression when used in the pregnant or postpartum populations. [67-69] In addition the PHQ9 is a valid instrument for perinatal depression screening. The use of PHQ-2 could precede PHQ-9 as a brief screening tool for perinatal depression in obstetric settings.[70]

DECISION ANALYSIS FOR TREATING THE PARTURIENT WOMAN

Despite the similar prevalence of antepartum depression to subsequent postpartum depression, the evidence for efficacy of treatment of antepartum depression is limited. The modification of interpersonal therapy for depressed antepartum women has been demonstrated to be feasible, effective and promising in the treatment of antenatal depression. Our trials of Interpersonal Psychotherapy for antepartum depression (IPT-P) were the first controlled treatment trials to demonstrate efficacy for pregnant depressed women.[32]

Since therapeutic guidelines dictate the use of a least invasive effective treatment to protect mother and fetus, a risk/benefit evaluation is the appropriate method for intervention. Decision analysis guides appropriate management. The initial step in the decision process is to determine the risk of untreated illness during pregnancy and consider factors which compromise fetal development.

The next step in the process is consideration of treatment risk. Although SSRIs and some other antidepressants have demonstrated relative safety during gestation absolute safety cannot be assured.[72] Electroconvulsive therapy is generally regarded as a safe and effective treatment during pregnancy for some psychiatric disorders and often indicated for psychotic mood disorders, severe depression or catatonia. ECT is also used for psychiatric emergencies or to replace failed treatments. Clinical guidelines exist.[73] Limited pilot data exists on non-pharmacological treatments of antepartum depression such as transcranial magnetic stimulation[74] and light therapy.[75]

There is a considerable literature on the treatment of postpartum depression with medication. The decision analysis for postpartum depression considers several factors. The first factor to affect the treatment decision is breastfeeding. Although there is a minimal amount of drug in the mother's milk for most antidepressants, a woman may hesitate to use medication while breastfeeding. Even mothers using formula may choose not to use medication. If depression were mild or moderate, IPT-P would be the treatment of choice. The efficacy of IPT for postpartum depression has been demonstrated.[41]

The benefit of psychotherapy has been a central theme of recent antidepressant trials. Keller et al.[76] demonstrated the efficacy of combined cognitive behavioral psychotherapy (CBT) and pharmacotherapy over either treatment alone. Psychotherapy provides an opportunity to explore conflicts, and develop coping patterns for the changes and developmental tasks of pregnancy.[4] Increased dependency may cause anxiety in a woman who, because of career interruption, fears losing her identity. Psychotherapy addresses impending separation from the infant, loss of independence, as well as the new alliance between husband and patient.

Several clinical trials have demonstrated the efficacy of IPT in depressed patients. The benefits of psychotherapy are associated with brain and physiological changes. Brody et al (1999) [39] found an increase in metabolic activity of the inferior frontal gyrus and the anterior insula for subjects treated with IPT compared to controls.

This application of IPT-P to the specific problems and needs of women with perinatal depression is manualized using guidelines and modifications around the issues of pregnancy. IPT-P addresses psychosocial concerns and stressors of parturition. This manual adds to modifications in the postpartum period. Clinicians in the U.S., Canada, Australia, U.K., Europe, South America and South Africa currently use the manual as a guide for treatment.

GUIDELINES FOR INTERPERSONAL PSYCHOTHERAPY

The goals of IPT include 1) decreased symptoms of depression and 2) resolution of interpersonal difficulties.[32] IPT emphasizes the possibility that depression occurs in an interpersonal context, but interpersonal issues are not considered the cause of depression.

In addition to biological change, peripartum women have significant stressors, i.e., changing role in society and family, concerns over obstetric difficulties, and acceptance of the parental role. IPT-P is designed to enable the patient to cope with interpersonal problems associated with symptom onset.

The three-tiered conceptual framework of IPT-P: [32]
1. Symptom formation: includes both biological and psychological etiology.
2. Social functioning: Social interaction with others is derived from early attachments, psychological experiences and current social functioning. Additional issues include maternal attachment to the infant.
3. Personality: enduring character traits may challenge coping skills and precipitate symptom onset.

Strategies of IPT are separated into 3 phases of treatment. The initial phase is comprised of collecting an interpersonal inventory of relationships, psychoeducation about IPT-P and depression and selection of problem areas for treatment. The medical model is used and depression discussed as a biological illness. The major issues associated with depression are identified. The patient and therapist agree on the framework of the treatment and the selected problem area.

In the intermediate phase, the work of IPT-P the therapist and patient identify one or two of five problem areas associated with depression. Four areas to include 1) grief, 2) role dispute, 3) role transition, and 4) interpersonal deficits. [32] IPT-P modified for the perinatal patient has one additional area of focus, the complicated pregnancy. Focus of treatment is in the present with reference to past relationships only as they relate to or parallel the present relationships. The work of IPT-P begins with emphasis on the patient's particular problem, as it is associated with depression. In termination phase progress is discussed, application of learned skills for future work is reviewed and feelings about termination are examined.

If the patient delivers before the completion of the 12 weeks of IPT-P course of treatment, the psychotherapy is later resumed or appropriate treatment selected. After delivery, the patient is evaluated monthly for 6 months to determine current status of depression during the postnatal period. This extends into the period of early parenting and permits evaluation of postpartum mood and mother-infant interaction.

This IPT-P manual is modified to address the issue of role transition, the developmental stages of pregnancy and the interpersonal issues related to the spouse, children and the woman's own parents as it effects her parenting role. In addition, the demands on the patient's time, occasional need for bed rest and delivery may require more scheduling flexibility and phone or Skype sessions for perinatal patients. In view of the role transition for both parents, couple's sessions are encouraged.

INITIAL EVALUATION OF PERINATAL WOMAN

Although initial sessions should be focused, the patient should be permitted to present symptoms including a history of present illness, duration of symptoms and the reason why she presents at this time. The patient should have a recent physical examination by her obstetrician including routine laboratory and thyroid function tests.

Past psychiatric history should include time and duration of past episodes of depression, treatment modalities, interpersonal precipitants or subsequent difficulties. Both medical and obstetric histories are reviewed. The seriousness of depression is evaluated, and suicidal intent is assessed. The risk/benefit of pharmacotherapy must also be evaluated and discussed with the patient.

The patient is then educated about the biological and psychosocial etiologies of depression. In addition, symptoms must be reviewed in detail.[32] Often this reassures the patient that she is not "crazy", that her fatigue, sleepiness, leaden paralysis, poor bonding and sensitivity to criticism are attributable to her depression. The patient should be reassured that disconnection or negative feelings toward the fetus or infant may occur in depression.

The therapist should convey to the patient that depression is a time-limited and treatable illness and that she is not to blame for the circumstances. Review of symptoms is reported[32] with some modification to the parturient woman. Depressive symptoms may mimic the discomforts of the pregnant and postpartum woman.

A review of symptoms and mild discomforts and mild discomforts include:
1st Trimester: fatigue, hypersomnia, anergia, nausea, vomiting, appetite change, mood lability and frequent urination
2nd Trimester: fetal movement occurs/improved somatic symptoms
3rd Trimester: fatigue, anergia, and frequent urination returns. Insomnia may be secondary to movements of the baby.

DIFFERENTIATING PREGNANCY DISCOMFORTS FROM DEPRESSIVE SYMPTOMS: [32] REVIEW OF SYMPTOMS IN THE CLINICAL INTERVIEW:

- *Depressed mood: Is the patient sad or tearful? What is the duration of the symptoms? Did they begin before pregnancy or after? Describe how you are feeling. Do you feel helpless? How do you feel about the pregnancy, the baby, the future? Can you see yourself getting better?*
- *Feelings of Guilt: Are you blaming yourself for things? Do these thoughts recur like ruminations? Do you feel you are not now, or will not be a good mother? Do you think that you are a "bad mother?" Do you feel badly that you are not excited about the baby, and therefore, are not living up to people's expectations? Do you think you have a boy or girl? Have you chosen a name?*
- *Suicide: Do you feel that life is not worth living? Do you have thoughts or plans of death? Would you call me if you felt you might hurt yourself? Have you ever made a suicide attempt? Who will care for your children if you are not there? What would keep you from hurting yourself?*
- *Infanticide: Do you worry that you migh*t hurt your baby? Do you feel angry or hostile toward the fetus or infant? Do you have intrusive thoughts or fear of harming your baby?
- *Insomnia:* Are you having trouble falling asleep or staying asleep? Do you wake during the night, or too early in the morning? How long do you lie awake? Can you attribute these problems to the baby's movement or anxiety? What do you think about when you are lying awake? Do you get up during the night to urinate? Do you return to sleep easily? If postpartum, can you sleep when the baby sleeps?
- *Social and Occupational Functioning:* Have you missed work? Are you less interested in your job now than before? Do you know why? Are you socializing? Is it hard to get started in the morning? Can you manage the other children? Are you easily irritated with them? If postpartum, do you feel bonded to your baby?
- *Retardation:* Psychomotor activity should be assessed during the evaluation while attending to limited movement with time of gestation and girth of the mother. Postpartum women may also have limited movement. Are her movements slow? Is the speech slow or low volume? Assess thought process along with concentration during the evaluation.
- *Agitation:* This should be rated during the interview. Is this woman restless, and is this

restlessness associated with anxiety? Is she able to sit still?

- *Psychic Anxiety:* Have you been nervous or frightened? How are you feeling about the delivery, about becoming a mother? Assess whether or not these fears are out of proportion to the real event. Do you feel something is wrong with the baby? Are you constantly checking to see if the baby is breathing?
- *Dissociative Symptoms:* Do you feel numb? Do you feel like you exist outside of yourself? Do you feel you are not really present? Do you feel unreal?
- *Paranoid Symptoms:* Are you suspicious of others? Do you feel people are talking about you?
- *Obsessional and Compulsive Symptoms:* Do you feel you must keep checking things? Do you feel you must perform actions in a special order? Do you worry over contamination? Do unpleasant or frightening thoughts come to your mind? Are you frightened that you might commit some terrible act without wanting to? Do you have fears that you may harm the baby? Do you have flashing images of harm to baby or others? Are you over concerned about contamination? Particularly as it applies to your baby?
- *Psychotic symptoms:* Do you hear voices, see images? Do you believe that you have special powers?
- *Trauma History:* Have you ever-experienced physical abuse? Have you ever experienced unwanted sexual touching?
- *Intimate Partner Violence:* Is your partner hitting, pushing you? Does he put you down or treat you badly in any way?
- *Somatic Anxiety:* Have you had any severe tremors or excessive sweating, shortness of breath, fainting or dizziness? It must be determined whether or not these conditions are associated with pregnancy, childbirth or have any other physiological cause such as dehydration, anemia or orthostatic hypotension.
- These symptoms may be associated with somatic anxiety common to the anxious patient:
  - G.I: Appetite? Bowel movement? Constipation is a frequent problem in pregnancy. Nausea and vomiting?
  - Cardiovascular: Palpitations? Tachycardia?
  - Genitourinary: Frequency? Frequent urination is a common symptom during the first and third trimester of pregnancy.
  - General Somatic Symptoms: Do you tire easily? Do you sleep more than usual? Do you stay in bed more than usual? Fatigue is a common symptom in the first and third trimester and after childbirth. Do you have many aches and pains? Are these associated with pregnancy? Do your arms and legs feel heavy?
  - Sexual Symptoms: How is your sex drive? Do you have orgasms? Third trimester and postpartum sexual activity may be uncomfortable, and should be accounted for.

- Attitudes Toward Body Complaints? Are they the main complaint in the evaluation? Does she obsess about them? Are they associated with pregnancy or childbirth?
- Weight Loss or Excessive Weight Gain: How much weight have you gained in the pregnancy? What does your obstetrician say? Have you lost weight?
- Insight? Do you believe that you are depressed? Do you feel that God is punishing you? Do you blame the baby for your depression?
- Diurnal Variation: Do you feel worse in the morning, and better in the evening or vice versa?

PHASES OF IPT-P TREATMENT

IPT-P has been adapted to treat patients with depressive symptoms that occur during pregnancy. The patient cannot be actively suicidal, psychotic or actively abusing alcohol or drugs. During the initial phase of treatment, depressive symptoms are noted and monitored weekly. Psychoeducation is begun and an interpersonal inventory is collected. Identifying both a problem area and also the focus of treatment will be the substance of the treatment contract with the patient.

INITIAL PHASE:

During the initial phase of treatment (weeks 1-4) the therapist should accomplish the following tasks described by Klerman, Weissman et al.[32]

1. Diagnose the depressive disorder.
2. Assess suitability for treatment and feasibility of coming to session with some flexibility around childbirth issues.
3. Conduct a formal interpersonal inventory of significant others in the patient's life. Determine the interaction between the patient and significant others, style of communication and feelings about pregnancy and the infant. Identify parallels in relationships. Relate these interpersonal difficulties to depressive symptoms.
4. Identify principal problem areas.
5. Explain the rationale for interpersonal therapy, and outline the progress of treatment over the sessions
6. Make a treatment contract with the patient
7. Explain the patient's role in the treatment
8. Begin treating symptoms

TASKS OF THE INITIAL PHASE OF IPT-P:

1. *Diagnose the depressive disorder:*
   Described above in section D using DSM-V then get baseline scores on HDRS, EPDS or PHQ.
2. *Assess Suitability for IPT:*

Although IPT-P appears to be ideal for most pregnant women, it may not be appropriate for all. Most women prefer to avoid medication during gestation. This may provide the necessary motivation for a woman to seek IPT-P intervention. In addition, the IPT-P therapist is often a welcome support during a time of high anxiety. Many women have fears, questions, and concerns, particularly if it is a first pregnancy. Because IPT-P does not explore issues psychodynamically, [32] women with personality disorders may not benefit with this form of therapy. For example, the patient with narcissistic character pathology may be unable to tolerate direct confrontation. The IPT-P therapist must be sensitive to the patient's ability to tolerate the style of the IPT-P therapist.

3.   *Circumstances of Conception and Pregnancy:*
For the married woman with all of the financial, social and emotional supports in place, a planned pregnancy is a wonderful event. However, many women who conceive decide to continue the pregnancy, but have no significant other. Some experience a break in the relationship that fostered the pregnancy. Under the best of circumstances, women may feel ambivalent about pregnancy, and have concerns about childbirth. Under the worst of circumstances, the depressed woman without supports simply may feel overwhelmed.

4.   *The Formal Interpersonal Inventory*[32]:
The next step for the IPT-P therapist is a discussion of significant relationships in the patient's life. Overall concentration is on present relationships. The past, however, should be explored particularly as it relates to the present life circumstances. Enduring patterns, as well as dysfunction, should be explored and addressed. The role of the baby's father is obvious and may in fact determine the mood and the outcome of the pregnancy. If the father is non-supportive, unavailable or absent the problem must be addressed during the treatment in the form of role dispute or grief. The relationship with the infant also should be explored. Feelings may range from joy, to ambivalence, to disguised or even overt hostility. This critical information must be explored in the therapy. These feelings should be addressed in a nonjudgmental and supportive way so that the patient can share them openly. Negative feelings must be attended to as delivery approaches because hidden shameful feelings may fester and culminate in poor mother-infant interaction, child abuse or in extreme scenarios, infanticide. Relationships with a new baby, and other children should be explored. Does the mother enjoy her children? Is she overwhelmed, angry or isolated? What method of discipline is used?

5.   *Identify Principal Problem Areas:*
Important problem areas should relate to depressive symptoms, although they may be neither the cause nor the result of the depression. The problem area for treatment is best approached when the patient and the therapist are in accord. The areas of focus include role dispute, grief, role transition, interpersonal deficits and complicated pregnancy.

6.   *Explain Rational and Progress of Treatment:*
The patient should have a good understanding of the theory of IPT-P, and how it relates to

depression. The course, timing and duration of appointments should be clearly explained, and feasibility of treatment explored. The policy for broken appointments, flexibility during such times as bed rest, hospitalization or childcare are important points of discussion.

7.   *Treatment Contract:*
The optimum time for establishing a contract between patient and therapist is in these early sessions. Agreement should be reached on such issues as time and duration of appointments. A financial contract, which includes a fee for broken appointments and notice-of-cancellation requirements, must be discussed. The patient should be assured that all information is confidential. She should be advised of the brief therapy time frame, and the specific time limit for the treatment.

8.   *Patient's role in treatment:*
The patient should be assured that her depression is not her fault. The patient must understand that she is free to discuss anything in the treatment. She is encouraged to begin discussions in sessions. She must be encouraged to take the "sick role" and permit herself the caring that she has not received during this illness.[32, 77] This may be difficult for the mother with small children at home. She should be encouraged to rest whenever possible. Depression is presented as a biological illness through the use of verbal and picture representations. Analogies are made to other medical illnesses such as diabetes or pneumonia.

BEGIN PSYCHOTHERAPY:

THE MIDDLE PHASE OF IPT-P TREATMENT:

The practice of psychotherapy with a pregnant and postpartum women[77] is a unique experience. The pregnant woman has an active fantasy life as well as a unique capacity for insight. Physiological processes and fetal growth place a large toll on her emotional life. The pressure to achieve stability or emotional equilibrium before birth and the rapid absorption of psychological change increase the toll.

While pregnant, the woman is mobile and free to look after herself. The motivation to be a good mother is high, as is the motivation to explore her own strengths and resources. But the built-in termination date of the baby's birth invokes an urgent sense to achieve stability before delivery.[60] Similarly, the new postpartum mother is enthusiastic about maintaining her own mental health to provide optimum mothering for her baby.

This middle phase of IPT-P is the active phase of therapy. The patient is encouraged to open sessions. It is during the middle phase that important issues are explained and strategies for working through problems are discussed. While the initial phase has focused on assessment by the therapist, the middle sessions now shift responsibility from the therapist to the patient. The patient is encouraged to give up her "sick role", to actively bring the focus of the therapy into the sessions, and to be open to exploration.

Tasks of the therapist: [32]
1. *Monitor symptoms, discuss with patient and evaluate need for adjunctive therapy*
2. *If infant is present, monitor bonding and interaction of mother and baby*
3. *Encourage the patient to open sessions and discuss issues relevant to the identified problem area*
4. *Identify feelings expressed by the patient particularly those associated with the chosen area of focus*
5. *Maintain flexibility. If necessary or helpful, permit significant others into sessions*
6. *Assist the patient to identify conflicts in the maternal role as it relates to the problem area*

Role of the Patient:
The patient is expected to take a more active role in the middle phase of the treatment. She progresses beyond the interpersonal inventory. Symptoms are regularly reviewed with the patient. The patient discusses feelings then the patient and the therapist explore those associated with the problem areas. The therapist encourages the patient's forward movement and life activities (exercising, meditation, movies) remaining empathic to the patient's mood.

The Role of the Therapist:
During this phase, the therapist encourages the patient to discuss feelings and facilitates their association with issues in the treatment.[77] The therapist must evaluate the progress, the need for adjunctive treatment and the need to continue or alter the problem area. Monitoring depressive symptoms is an ongoing process, with a formal review of symptoms taking place at the beginning of each session. HDRS or EPDS is completed and reviewed at each session.

Addressing the Problem Areas:
The patient should be permitted and encouraged to begin the session, introducing the subject that she deems important. If she is unable to begin, the therapist can begin the session by asking about recent issues or problems in the past week. The material should be relevant and focus on the present problem area. She should be regularly redirected back to the present material and problem area. At the conclusion of the session the therapist can summarize the session bringing attention to the problem area.

Therapist-Patient Relationship:
The therapist must be mindful both of the developing relationship between the patient and the therapist, and mindful of countertransference feelings.[78] The therapist must be attuned to the patient's verbal and nonverbal reactions and feelings, and encourage the patient to share these feelings. This is particularly important if the focus of treatment is interpersonal deficits. In this problem area, the patient-therapist relationship is the model for developing interpersonal skills.

Similar to psychodynamic psychotherapy, the interpersonal psychotherapist recognizes the transference and counter transference, although this is not explored as a central theme. The emphasis is always on the present, on current interpersonal relationships.

Involving Others in the Session:
The interpersonal nature of the treatment offers the possibility that others may be invited in for one or two sessions. In addition, psychoeducation of the nature of depression, a frequently neglected area for families, can help family members to understand and facilitate the patient's recovery. In IPT-P, this is particularly true of the baby's father, but may also include siblings. Childbearing is a role transition, which places demands on the entire family. Including the significant other is also an appropriate therapeutic intervention if a dispute has reached an impasse or if expectations differ. Bereavement will also affect the spouse, particularly if the loss was a perinatal one. It permits the therapist to observe the patient's interpersonal communication, feelings and coping. Although the therapist must be open to the inclusion of others in the session, such invitations require the consent of the patient. Confidentiality must be respected, and boundaries discussed before the joint session is held.

Managing a Crisis:
If the patient becomes overwhelmed and experiences impulsive suicidal feelings, this crisis takes precedence over any other treatment focus. After crisis resolution, the therapist can relate the crisis to the focus of treatment, which may expose new insights. Suicidal feelings should be evaluated at every session. Because the mother may deliver during treatment, it is also important to inquire about any destructive feelings that the mother may have towards the infant. Fears or thoughts of hurting the child must be explored and carefully differentiated from the wish to act on these feelings.

Keeping the Brief Treatment Time Frame:
The time frame of the treatment must be explained clearly, and the patient reminded weekly of the number of sessions remaining. The goals and strategies of the treatment should be reviewed. The therapist instills a sense of competence for the patient to use and develop these interpersonal skills in her everyday life.

The middle sessions of IPT-P concentrate on the process of change and development of interpersonal skills. Both therapist and patient are active in bringing feelings, issues and conflicts to the sessions. Although the therapist is the facilitator in this process, the patient should be encouraged to play the more active role, generating strategies and clarifying issues for future problem solving.

TERMINATION PHASE OF IPT-P TREATMENT:

The termination of treatment for the new mother can be complicated. If she has given birth before termination, her baby accompanies her in the final sessions. The patient faces the task of giving up her relationship with the therapist.[32] Emphasis should be placed on the patient's new sense of competence and abilities that have been discussed with the therapist. It is not unusual for depressive symptoms to return in the final days of therapy. The patient should be encouraged to explore recurrence of feelings and understand them as a consequence of the termination.

The task of termination, accomplished in the last 4 sessions[32] should include:
1. *Explicitly discussing the end of treatment*
2. *Acknowledging this as a time of potential grieving*
3. *Movement toward the recognition of her independent competence*

PROBLEM AREAS FOR TREATMENT

GRIEF

Grief is chosen as the problem area if the patient associates depression with death or loss. The loss may not have occurred at the same time as the depression. Grief may have been postponed or the lost one inadequately mourned.[32] This can be explored during initial sessions during the interpersonal inventory. Lewis & Casement[79] suggest that bereavement is not mourned appropriately during pregnancy because the mother is preoccupied with the new life inside her.

The normal grief reaction includes sensations of somatic distress, preoccupation with the image of the lost person, feelings of guilt and hostility, and change in the usual patterns of conduct[80.] Bereavement may be delayed or postponed indefinitely as a result of the patient's coping strategies or resistance.[81] Grief may manifest during a subsequent event in the patient's life such as birth, death or pregnancy. Manifestations of abnormal bereavement include overreacting, the development of somatic symptoms of the bereaved, exacerbations of pre-existing physical disorders, breakdowns in relationships, repressed hostility and rage, social withdrawal, self-destructive activities and agitated depression.

Abnormal grief reactions are of two types: delayed grief and distorted grief.[32]
In a *delayed grief reaction*, grieving is postponed for an indeterminate period of time. The grief may present later, but usually as depression. It may be triggered by life circumstances or other losses. The history of loss is identified during the interpersonal inventory, and can help to explain the genesis of this grief. The patient may not be aware of the connection of grief to the depression.
A *distorted grief reaction* may occur either immediately or be postponed to a later time. The reaction, inappropriate to the loss, may manifest itself as either indifference or somatic concerns. Lewis[81] describes the inhibition of mourning by pregnancy. He posits that bereavement is difficult because the woman is increasingly preoccupied with thoughts, fantasies and feelings about the new baby. Mourning, therefore, is interrupted. Because mourning requires a similar preoccupation with the deceased to become free from the loss, it is impossible to resume mourning at a later

time. This unresolved mourning might be activated later in time in pathological forms by events such as depression.

With incomplete mourning, the patient may identify with the lost loved one resulting in prolonged depression, hypochondriasis or somatic conversion. Feelings may be cut off, resulting in impaired bonding to the newborn. During mourning the bereaved unconsciously imagines the deceased to be absorbed into her mind and body. Because the mother's image of the unborn baby is poorly defined, she may confuse her feelings for the dead with those for her unborn child. The therapist must assist the mother to separate the image of her unborn child from the image of the deceased.

Fetal or perinatal loss presents a difficult and complicated emotional task for the mother. Historically, attempts were made to console the mother by suggesting that she could still have other children. It is now appropriate that maternal grief is facilitated rather than impeded or postponed. The mother may want to view or hold her dead infant. Naming the child, as well as conducting funeral services and burial rites may facilitate this mourning process.[82]

Complicated Grief: Mothers may blame themselves for the death of the child, feel angry over the injustice of the loss, and yearn to regain the dead child and devalue their maternal competency. Denial is a powerful defense, and often impedes the mourning of perinatal death. Factors such as guilt, dependency on the deceased or suddenness of the occurrence may prevent the resolution of mourning.

Factors other than death may also create feelings of loss. For the woman, pregnancy may mean loss of physical well-being, of positive body image, and of a more carefree social life. She must adjust to the idea of a postponed career, of potential financial and emotional instability and concern about the health of her infant. These factors contribute to the psychological distress of pregnancy and may also contribute to a grief reaction.

TREATMENT STRATEGIES FOR GRIEF

The goals of the IPT-P therapist are to facilitate the mourning process for the patient, and assist her in developing interests and relationships, which may substitute for her loss.[32] Feelings should be explored in a nonjudgmental manner in order to facilitate even ambivalent feelings, which the mother may have and be ashamed of. She should be reassured that she is in a safe environment and she need not fear feeling either out of control or unable to tolerate the affect.

The relationship with the deceased child or loved one should be reconstructed. If this is a fetal loss, reconstruction should be from the beginning of the pregnancy. All expressions of feelings should be encouraged, particularly ambivalence and hostility for which the patient may feel guilt. The patient should be assured that positive feelings will follow negative ones. She should be encouraged to see the relationship realistically. She should also be encouraged to develop other activities and relationships[32].

In the case of perinatal loss, there may be an unconscious selection of a subsequent child to replace the lost child. This new child may be identified with the deceased. Efforts should be made to separate the dead child's identity from the identity of the child chosen to replace the loss.

The patient must recognize this association with the deceased before the dead person's identity can be relinquished. Overprotection and anxiety may be the dominant features of the interaction with the new child. The mother must confront both her fears of another loss, and her anger that the replacement child cannot undo the loss of the deceased. Because the mother has either minimal or no interaction with the deceased child, her feelings are more easily displaced from the lost child to the subsequent pregnancy. The blow to self-worth may result in an eagerness to be pregnant again in order to repair the narcissistic damage. If mourning is incomplete, the subsequent child cannot be loved in his or her own right and will remain an unsatisfactory substitute for the lost child.

A woman with a history of spontaneous or induced abortions is also at risk for mood changes during pregnancy, particularly if she was ambivalent about termination. Often she will continue to feel guilty, and will have additional concerns about her infant's health and well-being. One other population who may suffer grief reactions is women with multiple gestations who have reduced the pregnancy in order to improve viability for the other infants.

The task of the IPT-P therapist is to facilitate expression of the mother's grief through empathic and nonjudgmental encouragement to share her feelings of sadness and loss. A patient's childhood deprivation or long-standing ambivalent feelings towards her own mother may also impede mourning. Because memories cannot be mounted for the loss of a newborn, the context of grief must be shared in the wishes, fantasies and hopes of a child who will never be. Termination will be crucial to the treatment, and will highlight how completely the death has been resolved.[82]

CASE VIGNETTE: GRIEF

The case of D:
D, a 25 year-old married female presents at 20 weeks gestation, describes the onset of depression in the past 3 weeks, soon after she felt her baby move. She and her husband were enthusiastic about the planned pregnancy.

At 17 years of age D became pregnant by her boyfriend. She shared the news with no one except him; She had a precipitous vaginal delivery in the ambulance on the way to the hospital. The infant died.

She refused to attend the burial. She and her baby's father never communicated again. She never spoke of the event and "put it out of her mind". D completed graduate school, had a successful career in advertising, married and planned a family.

In the initial session, D was depressed and tearful. She felt especially guilty and perplexed about her depression. She was so pleased about her pregnancy. She had guilty ruminations about the first baby, and felt responsible for her baby's death. D had hoped that this child would replace the first child, and that the guilt feelings would subside. They worsened. She feared she would be punished and lose this child. She never revealed the facts of her first pregnancy to her husband. She became somatically preoccupied, obsessed with fetal movements and worried that her own activity might endanger the baby. The therapeutic stance with the patient was supportive and non-judgmental. Reconstruction of her pregnancy, her initial reaction to the news, thoughts and feelings about the infant were discussed.

Initial Phase (sessions 1-4)

The patient initially described her guilt and shame over her first pregnancy. She believed that if she confided in someone and had prenatal care, her baby would have lived. She was able, by the 3rd session to describe her own mother who was hostile and withholding. She feared she would repeat this maternal behavior. She felt supported by her husband, but feared losing him if he knew about her past.

Middle Phase (sessions 5-8)

D revealed her ambivalence about her first pregnancy. She hoped that she would experience relief by replacing the lost infant. While she desired a pregnancy, she recognized her own feelings of ambivalence and hostility. D also described fantasies of her dead baby. Eventually, D told her husband about her first pregnancy and delivery. This required a couple's session. Despite feeling hurt, her husband was supportive, and assisted D in her mourning by escorting her to the never-before visited infant's grave.

Termination (sessions 8-12)

As therapy came to an end, the patient became asymptomatic. The termination of her treatment signaled final mourning for her baby. By giving her dead baby a final resting place in her memory, she was able to begin plans for the new child.

PREGNANCY AS A ROLE TRANSITION

Parenthood, and especially the period of pregnancy and motherhood is among the most common and complete transformations in human experience.[83] The woman becomes transformed both in her own image and the eyes of others. The external transformation is paralleled by both internal hormonal and psychological changes as well as the development of nurturing skills. Pregnancy, a time of developmental upheaval, is similar to the onset of adolescence or the passage of menopause. The woman's self-concept is reorganized as she adapts to her new role as mother. The process is completed with the psychological separation from the child.

A woman with a successful career may have difficulty changing her work habits and lifestyle. With the arrival of the child, she may indeed resent the intrusion of the infant. If she has a strong investment in her body image, the changing shape of her body may distress her. She may fear a disruption to the bond with her husband. These issues may cause the woman to become ambivalent and resentful about the potential changes in her life.

TREATMENT STRATEGIES FOR ROLE TRANSITION

Roles in society contribute to one's sense of self-esteem and identification.[32] If a person has difficulty coping with, or making the transition from one role to another, depression may be the outcome. Social functioning may be impaired while adapting to new roles, particularly if the old role is seen as a loss. This is evident in pregnancy and childbirth where the new role of mother is associated with a necessary loss of independence.

Difficulties in coping may manifest as:
1. *Loss of familiar social supports*
2. *Management of accompanying emotions, such as anger or fear*
3. *Demands for a new repertoire of social skills*
4. *Diminished self-esteem*

The tasks involved in mastering the role transition can be achieved only if the person had completed the tasks of the former role. In order to work through the transition, the therapist must assist the patient to explore the old role, and leave it behind. The patient must work through anger and loss, acquire new skills and acquire new supports for the future.

1. *Evaluation of Old Role:*
Similar to the grief experience, the old role should be explored, and the patient encouraged to place it in perspective. Most women approach pregnancy with some ambivalence even if the pregnancy was planned. The anxiety of pregnancy and childbirth reinforces the idealization of the old role with its familiarities attaching negative feelings to the new role. Both positive and negative aspects of the old role are explored. The patient is reassured that she does not have to relinquish all aspects of the old role. Although there is a loss of independence, it is important to recognize areas where the patient feels some control. For example, a graduate student may be able to work out childcare, take fewer courses, without giving up her plans for education.

2. *Encourage Affective Expression:*
Reassuring the patient that ambivalence is a normal experience in pregnancy even under the best and well-planned circumstances, may assist her in expressing her emotion. If the woman has achieved success and independence in her career, she may fear the loss of these important elements in her life and mourn her loss of stature. This may entail expressions of guilt because she feels the responsibility to be a "happy mother". Facilitating transition means eliciting feelings about the change.

3. *Developing New Social Skills:*
Coping skills should be evaluated, and the patient encouraged to use and develop them during the transition. The new skills necessary for the change such as parenting skills, or managing the care of 2 children instead of 1 can prove an awesome undertaking for the new mother. Incorrect assumptions about the new role should be explored and clarified ("I'm afraid that I will not be able to resume my career after the baby is born").

4. *Establishing Social Supports:*
Parenting is a learned process. Although some parents learn from modeling their own families, a woman from a dysfunctional family may be under-prepared to raise a child. She should be encouraged to form her own network of friends who are parents of young children, She should also be encouraged to attend parenting classes to help ease her apprehension and encourage

her to include her partner in this process.

CASE VIGNETTE: ROLE TRANSITION:

The case of P:

P, a 22 year-old, single primiparous college student in her 6th postpartum week was born in the United States and raised in the Dominican Republic. She had a long history of physical abuse by her father. She was living in one room of a family's apartment, supported by public assistance. She presented with depressive symptoms, which include tearfulness, anxiety, inability to sleep when the baby sleeps, poor appetite and weight loss. P conceived on a first date with a law student. She informed him of the pregnancy, and refused the abortion he offered to finance. She quit school, and lived without support from her family. She feared abusing her child as her father had abused her.

Initial Phase (Sessions 1-4)

P's concerns related to the anticipated birth. She felt that she could not terminate the pregnancy. Her depression developed after her delivery. Her history of abuse by her alcoholic father began when she attempted to save her mother from her father's assaultiveness. The abuse prompted a suicide attempt at the age of 12. The described brief sexual encounter prompted her to re-evaluate her own parenting, and her father's mistreatment. Her pregnancy was one of several re-victimizations that she sustained in her life. College was her way out, but the pregnancy and childbirth threatened her attendance.

Middle Phase (sessions 5-8)

When P began to explore the benefits of education, she realized she could continue even with her new baby. To ease her isolation, she joined a bible study group. She grieved the loss of independence and interrupted education. She explored avenues to allow her to continue school, and yet remain available for her child. Her symptoms diminished when she worked with her anger, disappointment, and unrealistic expectations of the baby's father who had not assumed parental responsibility.

Termination (sessions 8-12)

As treatment came to an end, P joined a parent-infant program which provided support and counseling for the mother-infant dyad. She came to realize that she could return to school successfully. The parent-infant program encouraged her to develop the coping skills to manage both her mothering and her part-time education.

INTERPERSONAL ROLE DISPUTE

A role dispute as one in which two people have conflicting expectations in their relationship.[32] An example is the pregnant woman who expects to stop work after her child is born and become a "full-time mother". Because of a change in her husband's earnings, she must resume work.

The IPT-P therapist should focus on a role dispute, which has occurred in the context of depression. A role dispute contributes to the patient's poor self-esteem and makes her feel both powerless and out of control. In addition, the possible loss of the relationship itself may be threatening. The couple may have reached an impasse or may have poor communication skills, which make them incapable of resolving conflicts.

The patient should relate overt difficulties in relationships, which coincide with depression. The cognitive impairment in depression predisposes the patient to feelings of failure and guilt. When completing the interpersonal inventory, the therapist should explore how relationships had changed both before and after the onset of depression.

TREATMENT STRATEGIES FOR ROLE DISPUTE

The patient should be encouraged to play an active role in the planned strategy. The therapist should help the patient illuminate the current dispute and then make plans for a program to modify communication and expectations. It is not the therapist's task to salvage a relationship. He/she should follow the patient's lead and explore a desirable and realistic outcome.

The stages of role dispute[32] which should be determined before active treatment begins:
1. *Renegotiation* suggests that the patient, husband or significant other are interested in working out difficulties and improving communication.
2. *Impasse* implies that the couple has stopped communicating, and the relationship is saddled with an undercurrent of anger.
3. *Dissolution* suggests that the couple has stopped trying to communicate, that they are disinterested in negotiation, and that the relationship is unsalvageable.

The role of the therapist is to assist the patient to understand her role expectations, to master negotiations, and assist resolution. I find that communication analysis is the most helpful modality. What are the issues in the dispute? What are values and expectations? Are these expectations realistic? What is the patient's capacity for personal change, as well as change in the relationship? Parallels in old relationships are explored. The patient is encouraged to express anger, as well as hurt and fear.

Disorders of Mother Infant Attachment as Role Dispute:
Although the concept of a role dispute with the infant may sound unusual, I have assigned mother-infant relationship disorders to the role dispute problem category. Hostile feelings toward the infant should be explored during gestation for the purpose of resolution before delivery. Pregnancy is a time of reawakening of repressed material that involves recall of the woman's own separation/individuation and relationship with her own parents. If the woman's own psychological dysfunction hampers her ability to express conflict or to create a relationship, the relationship with the fetus or infant will be impaired. If she has had a troubled early environment or unresolved conflicts, parenthood may be a time of turmoil. The infant may be viewed with hostility. If the

pregnancy was unexpected, the woman may feel resentful. She may view pregnancy as a source of envy, shame or pride. An unplanned pregnancy may be a source of anger directed at the fetus or the baby's father, or a source of fear if she has a history of a lost pregnancy or stillbirth.

Disorders of mother infant bond range from delayed attachment to infanticide.[84, 85] Approximately 10% of new mothers will have delayed attachment to their infant. Another 1% will have negative or hostile thoughts about their infant. Child abuse is also on the continuum of poor attachment. Although the bond to the infant may not be immediate, most will strengthen in the weeks after delivery. Although this is most often described in the postpartum period, these feelings can be detected during the pregnancy, and should be explored to assist the mother in the resolution of her hostile feelings.

Obsessional intrusive thoughts of the infant may also occur during gestation, but may not indicate rejection.[86] Rejection of the infant is usually found in unwanted pregnancies. It may also be detected in pregnancies where an amniocentesis has uncovered a congenital anomaly or genetic defect. This is complicated by the mother's own guilt, her anger and her feelings of failure which create hostile feelings toward the baby. The mother may feel trapped if it is too late to terminate the pregnancy and must therefore be assisted in resolving her hostility.

Often, delayed attachment resolves spontaneously in the days or weeks postpartum. Educating the woman during the prenatal period about delayed attachment may ease the burden and assist in resolution of the conflict. The mother should be encouraged to explore this relationship as it reflects the conflicts she has had with her own parents or with the infant's father. Delayed attachment can have significant sequelae such as failure to thrive, impaired emotional and cognitive development and difficulty developing relationships.[84] If attachment does not occur, the mother and infant should be referred for mother infant dyadic therapy. [87]

CASE VIGNETTE: INTERPERSONAL ROLE DISPUTE

The Case of R
R is a 22 year-old married, primiparous Hispanic female who presented at 24 weeks gestation with depression and marital problems in the preceding 3 months. Referred by her obstetrician for anxiety, anorexia and lack of weight gain, she complained of insomnia, obsessional ruminations and headaches. The patient had planned her pregnancy without her husband's knowledge, a source of anger, which was not discussed. This was particularly difficult because the husband was a new immigrant, unable to speak English or obtain reasonable work to support the family. When he lost his job, he became verbally and physically abusive. Another focus of dispute was the patient's exceedingly close relationship to her mother. She spent most days with her. In this case the focus of treatment was placed on 2 problem areas: 1) a role dispute with her husband to include improved communication and 2) role transition in her relationship with her mother, with focus on the couple.

Initial Phase (sessions 1-4)
The treatment strategy consisted of helping the patient to renegotiate her relationship with her

spouse. The patient accepted the sick role quite easily, and was able to understand that her unilateral impulsive decision to get pregnant without discussing it with her husband had been a serious blow to their relationship. Her depressive symptoms were related to disclosing the news of her pregnancy, and his abusive behavior. As the patient came to understand that her actions were wrong, it was important to stress the need for her own protection. Her depression was interpreted as her own anger turned inward because of guilt feelings. This left her feeling hopeless and helpless, and open to punishment.

Middle Phase (sessions 5-8)

The therapist tried to elicit descriptions of interactions between the patient and husband, and determine how their communication was experienced. Role-playing was crucial to demonstrate appropriate communication. One overriding concern was the abuse, which began before treatment. Once again, crisis management must take priority. The patient agreed that she would call the police if the abuse resumed. She tried to be more direct with her husband, and was pleased that he shared her interest in communicating. She was also able to focus on peer relationships, and was able to remove herself from her exceedingly dependent relationship with her mother.

Termination Phase (sessions 9-12)

This phase of treatment was particularly difficult because the patient had become dependent on both the therapist and the treatment. She was encouraged to use the treatment strategies independently. She also used her improved relationship with her husband for additional support. She was reminded that the work in therapy was hers. She was entitled to take credit, and leave therapy with acknowledgment of her own personal strengths. She understood that she could call the therapist if necessary.

COMPLICATED PREGNANCY AND CHILDBIRTH

Pregnancy and childbirth can be complicated by concurrent life events, such as a serious illness, obstetrical difficulties, and the death of a loved one or a previous perinatal loss. The pregnancy may have been undesired as the result of rape. Other complications may be successful conception after a period of infertility or multiple gestations.

Concurrent life-events:

The transition to motherhood may be encumbered by other transitional events such as moving to a new house or leaving a job. The additional stress and anxiety interrupt the psychological work of pregnancy as conflicting demands for readjustment are satisfied.

Stressors such as bereavement, job loss, the negative results of fetal diagnostic tests or a threatened miscarriage can invoke anxiety, grief, rejection and loss at a time when all expectations are of happiness and fulfillment. Conflicting feelings must be integrated, and the mother enabled to work towards their resolution, while sustaining the hopefulness of pregnancy.

Conflicted Pregnancy:

Conflicted pregnancy, refers to unplanned, untimely, and wrong or overvalued pregnancy. Overvalued pregnancies are the result of prolonged efforts to conceive such as infertility treatment, IVF, previous stillbirth, habitual spontaneous abortions or perinatal death. Ambivalence is manifested when the mother-to-be vacillates between hope and distrust, elation and detachment, idealization and nihilism. These women will become overanxious parents who will monitor the infant's every move and breath.

Unsupported women who find themselves alone after divorce, abandonment or the death of the partner are also highly distressed. They lack the feeling of control over their own destinies. Their grief, fear, guilt, resentment, sadness and fragility conflict with the expectation of a happy pregnancy. These feelings must be resolved and disentangled before the birth or the child may bear the brunt of unresolved "baggage". The mother may feel that the child has caused the break with the partner and this may be unconsciously conveyed to the child.

Unplanned pregnancy:

A woman on her own with an unplanned pregnancy must reevaluate her single identity and decide if she would like another person in her life for the next 20 years. The decision may entail moral, emotional and financial dilemmas as well as the complication of career demands. A fragile relationship may go into crisis. A well-established marriage may suddenly experience discord. Some partners in an unplanned pregnancy will accept the consequences of pregnancy, but do so only with considerable ambivalence.

Untimely pregnancy:

This may refer to a mother who is young, and associated with an interrupted adolescence, or a mother who is older who may have concerns over interruption in lifestyle and an increase in the risk of birth defects.

Wrong Pregnancy/Wrong father:

A pregnancy that results from rape or incest is complex on many levels including concern over the baby's normality, the future of the family and internalized feelings of blame and badness. If the woman continues the pregnancy, she has the task of differentiating between the baby and the rape. The baby will always be a reminder.

Wrong mother:

The woman or her partner may lack ability to parent well because of his or her own lack of proper nurturance or adequate mothering.

Rape:

The case of A:

A is a 21 year-old single black, unemployed primipara who presented with the onset of depressive symptoms for two months. Pregnancy was the outcome of a rape by her boyfriend. The patient had a history of sexual abuse and a terminated pregnancy secondary to a rape at 14 years old. She had no means of financial support and few other social supports. IPT-P focused on her dispute with the baby's father, her anger and lack of financial and emotional support. A was able to identify her anger, and assert herself for her own needs as well as those of her baby eventually pressing criminal charges against the rapist.

Concurrent Illness:

In general, the woman is significantly more anxious during pregnancy than she is during her prepregnant state. She is increasingly introspective and preoccupied with the pregnancy. She may also have heightened dependency needs[88]. Psychiatric disorders during pregnancy may be exacerbated or the woman may conversely have an increased period of well-being. Exacerbated psychiatric disorders may cause poor prenatal care, poor nutritional habits, fetal abuse or neonaticide. Schizophrenia is associated with obstetric complications.

Iancu[89] describes that 0.5-1.0 in 1000 women will develop severe and intractable nausea and vomiting in the first trimester of pregnancy. Hyperemesis gravidarum is characterized by dehydration, weight loss, electrolyte imbalance, ketosis, and liver or renal damage. Poor study methodology has resulted in little knowledge of psychological and physiological causes.[9] Early psychological intervention may contribute to the well-being of these women.

For the most part, infectious diseases do not seriously affect the pregnant woman or her fetus. There are however, some infectious diseases that have serious or life threatening consequences for the pregnant woman. Rubella (German measles) contracted during the first 4 months of gestation may result in congenital defects or even fetal death. Infants who survive have prolonged active viral infections.[90]

Diabetes mellitus places a significant burden upon the pregnant woman. Diabetes may either be pre-existing or may be precipitated by the pregnancy. Complications may include disturbed water balance, hypertension or pre-eclampsia, macrosomia (excessively large infant), stillbirth or neonatal death. These pregnant women must deal with both their anger at being cheated of a normal pregnancy as well as consequent fears about the outcome of the pregnancy, delivery, and need for education such as insulin self-administration.

Women with cardiac illness pose a significant risk during pregnancy. The high risk prenatal care includes frequent monitoring, the need for medications to control cardiac symptoms while carefully weighing the potential risk to the fetus[67], the possible need for bedrest and potential cardiac decompensation. Other chronic illnesses such as epilepsy, multiple sclerosis, lupus erythematosis and even neoplasms pose similar and obvious complications specific to their treatments.

Late pregnancy may present any type of vaginal bleeding although not all are of serious concern. The causes of vaginal bleeding are varied. Placenta praevia is the premature separation of an abnormally implanted placenta with consequent hemorrhage.[90] The seriousness is determined by the position of the placenta and covering of the cervical opening, Such factors will determine treatment. These may vary from bedrest to elective termination by cesarean section. Bleeding accompanied by pain may indicate abruptio placenta, and presents a need for emergency delivery.

The high-risk pregnant patient presents a host of complex problems. The risks and benefits consequent to diagnostic tests and treatment to both mother and fetus must be addressed. There do exist physiological implications of any disease for mother and fetus. These include the risks and benefits of diagnostic tests and medications, as well as the effects of gestational hormonal shifts on the course of disease at a time when physiology and metabolism are rapidly changing.

Fetal Anomalies:

The emotional consequences of giving birth to a defective child can be devastating.[91] Fetal anomalies may be detected with the use of amniocentesis accompanied by genetic counseling. The emotional trauma of losing a desired pregnancy or adapting to life with a child with a defect is often overwhelming. The couple may feel defective and suffer a blow to their self-esteem. The initial reaction is one of shock and disbelief, then anger, and finally grief and/or depression.

Selective termination may be sought when the mother has a multiple pregnancy. This may be done if one or more fetuses are abnormal or when continuation of the pregnancy poses a serious risk to the mother or to the pregnancy itself. This is most likely in infertility patients who now have multiple gestations due to ovulation induction

CASE VIGNETTE: COMPLICATED PREGNANCY:

The case of P

P was a 32 year-old multiparous female at 16 weeks gestation recently found to be seropositive for HIV. She contracted the disease from her husband, an IV drug abuser. She complained of uncontrollable anxiety, depressed mood, insomnia and anorexia. P was concerned about her own health, as well as that of her two other children. Her husband, already diagnosed with AIDS, had been hospitalized. The initial task of IPT-P was to assist P in coping with both the overwhelming news, as well as the uncertain future of her family.

Initial Phase (sessions 1-4)

P's depression was precipitated by the news of her HIV+ diagnosis. She was angry with her husband, and worried about the danger to her unborn child. The welfare of her other children weighed heavily as well. P needed time to see herself in the "sick role" before she could take on the role of caretaker for her family. She had been her husband's caretaker, and remained loyal to him despite his drug dependence. She wanted to leave him because of his abusiveness, but felt responsible for him because of his illness. P engaged the help of her mother who agreed to move in and care for the other children until P was feeling better. She also engaged the help of a social worker in order to obtain support for the children. She eventually separated from her husband.

Middle Phase (sessions 5-8)

P felt mildly improved after the separation. As she related her marital difficulties, she was able to identify her feelings. She made plans for childcare, finances and prenatal care. She began to re-establish old friendships, which had been suspended because of the problems in her marriage. Several sessions were spent developing her relationship with her children. With education, she began to understand that her HIV+ status was not a death sentence and she found appropriate support systems.

Termination Phase (sessions 13-16)

As termination grew near, P verbalized feelings of loneliness and isolation. She was encouraged to find strength in her support groups and did so as she prepared to separate from her therapist. She also joined a group of HIV+ pregnant woman who were living productive lives despite their seropositivity.

INTERPERSONAL DEFICITS

If the patient is socially impoverished with few, if any lasting relationships and has a history of extreme social isolation, personality deficits must be considered as treatment focus. The relationship with the therapist, rather than significant others will become the model for interaction.

TREATMENT STRATEGIES FOR INTERPERSONAL DEFICITS

The challenge of the treatment is to minimize social isolation[32]. Because there is an absence of relationships, old relationships will become the focus of treatment.

Klerman, Weissman and colleagues[32] have described the three tasks involved in handling a problem of interpersonal deficits:

  1. Review negative and positive aspects of past significant relationships
  2. Explore repetitive problems in these relationships
  3. Discuss negative and positive feelings about the therapist, and parallels in other relationships.

These socially impoverished patients require a more complete past personal inventory including any romantic relationships or childhood friends. The best and worst of each relationship are explored. Failed relationships are explored. Eventually more recent relationships are explored. Often the parental relationship provides the springboard for exploring the lifelong pattern of interactions. The history of the patient's role in the family often reveals how the patient views herself in the world. If, for example, she has few if any close friends, it may be a response to rejection or criticism.

If the patient has difficulty expressing anger, she may "act out" this anger outside of treatment. Such patients can be taught appropriate means of expressing their feelings through the model of the therapist-patient relationship where the most direct data about the patient will be provided. Solving problems, negotiating treatment contracts and co-operating with the therapist provides a useful model for the patient in the development of future relationships. Participation in role-playing may be an important modality in these patients. A referral for mother infant dyadic therapy is absolutely necessary.

CASE VIGNETTE: INTERPERSONAL DEFICITS:

The case of M:

M is 39 year-old divorced Hispanic female referred by her obstetrician for depressed mood and social withdrawal. The onset of depression coincided with the discovery of her pregnancy and was associated with recurrent thoughts of sexual abuse by a 16 year-old cousin who raped her when she was 6 years old. Her parents ignored her complaints. The patient correctly realized that this event had a significant impact on both her life and subsequent relationships.The baby's father was a janitor with whom the patient had little contact. He provided neither emotional nor financial support. She had no close friends or family. Her mother lived in the Dominican Republic

Initial Phase (Sessions 1-4)

During the initial evaluation and subsequent visits the patient never smiled, had a low monotone voice and a flat affect. The patient was reluctant to form close relationships because she feared disappointment. This theme paralleled her own formative experiences and describes the ongoing family dynamic. The patient's boyfriend was an alcoholic. He often "showed up" and although they barely spoke, they would have sexual intercourse. She passively agreed. Fearing intimacy and attachment, she felt this relationship would place no demands on her beyond the sexual contract.

Although the patient has always been detached from her mother, she remained close to her alcoholic father. The theme is similar to that described by her relationship with her boyfriend, a man who lacked the capacity to be emotionally involved or available. As a child she protected her father when he drank excessively. Although she succeeded in school, she was always socially isolated.

Middle Phase (sessions 5-8):

M explored her past relationships, clarified perceptions of her mother and her role as her father's protector. She identified positive experiences with the parents to use as models of future relationships. She examined her memories of the father who was affectionate when drinking, but never lived up to her expectations, or satisfied her needs as a child.

We explored the patient-therapist relationship to use as the model to modify future relationships. The patient, feeling better and working hard, missed 2 consecutive appointments after the therapist returned from vacation. When confronted with missed appointments, the patient confessed that the vacation had disturbed her. We explored M's difficulty fulfilling her own needs.

This opened the discussion of some recent friendships as well as the patient's sensitivity to rejection. She had poor self-esteem, and often sought or misinterpreted criticism. For example, she would improperly interpret the therapist's feelings. As this interpretation was exposed, she was able to express her hurt and anger without fearing retaliation. She eventually took steps outside of therapy with acquaintances at work and even asked co-workers to join her for lunch. She was able to interact with other mothers and made "play dates" with them for her baby.

Termination (sessions 9-12)

As termination of therapy neared, M became concerned that she would not be able to maintain her improved mood. She became angry and depressed. The therapist had informed M that she might experience a recurrence of her original symptoms so she was prepared for the end of therapy. She could not understand why she felt so angry with the therapist. Later she understood that her sadness was an extension of her feelings of abandonment. Reassured that she could continue the work independently, she was also reassured that she could call the therapist if a matter was urgent. M was encouraged to use her new IPT-P skills in her professional and social life. Her symptoms abated. She attended dyadic therapy and joined a mother-infant group after the baby was born.

SPECIFIC PSYCHOTHERAPY TECHNIQUES

Several psychotherapy techniques may apply to IPT.[32] Most therapists with psychodynamic training will be familiar with these techniques. Techniques are combined as appropriate to the treatment, the patient, the relationship of the therapist to the patient, and the situation at hand.

Exploratory Techniques:

Exploration consists of gathering information about the patient's symptoms and presenting problem. Open-ended questions and neutrality of the therapist facilitate disclosure and discussion. If such exploration is productive, the therapist may encourage the patient by supporting and acknowledging material, expanding the subject matter, receptive silence and or asking direct questions.

Encouragement of Affect:

Expressing affect brings feelings into awareness so that the patient can explore and tolerate them. Working with affect brings about change in psychotherapy. Three strategies are pursued: encouraging the patient to tolerate painful feelings, attend to the importance of affect in interpersonal relationships and helping the patient express suppressed feelings.

Clarification:

Clarification reorganizes the patient's words to make them aware of what they actually said. It provides a thoughtful and clear way to express what the patient is conveying such as contradictions or internal conflicts. One might ask the patient to repeat what they said. The therapist may restructure the content in order to clarify what was said. This is often used when the patient is discussing an unhelpful belief or thought.

Communication Analysis:

Communication analysis is like taking a microscope to discussions in order to identify failures in communication and facilitate understanding. It is useful to request detailed accounts of information presented. This may facilitate communication in a patient who is ambiguous, or lacks ability for direct confrontation or assumes information without clarification. Communication analysis is aimed at identifying communication failures, and guiding the patient towards more effective communication. The therapist should listen for assumptions, thoughts, feelings, and incorrect expectations. Details of particular conversations or disputes must be reviewed.

Use of the Therapeutic Relationship:

The relationship between the therapist and patient should serve as a model for relationships outside of treatment. Thoughts, feelings and body language may be identified. Communication analysis is a "here and now" example of interpersonal difficulties. The patient should be encouraged to express feelings about the therapist to assist the therapist in correcting both distortions and other problems in treatment. This data might also be used to correct distorted views of others.

Behavior Change Techniques: [32]

The treatment of depression is based on the successful changes in interpersonal relationships outside of therapy. In IPT-P the therapist can use directive techniques, decision analysis and role-playing to facilitate behavior change. *Directive Techniques:* These techniques include interventions such as education, advice, modeling and direct help to the patient in order to solve practical problems. The patient may be assisted in finding childcare, financial aid and other strategic necessities. Rather than direct assistance in these matters, the patient should be guided to analyze new situations and make decisions. The therapist should progress from direct interventions to the encouragement of the patient's independence. Direct techniques should be used sparingly, in order to assist the patient in choosing options rather than have the decision made for her. *Decision Analysis* facilitates consideration of appropriate options.

PROBLEMS ENCOUNTERED IN THE THERAPY:

I include the valuable list of problems described by Klerman, Weissman et al.

The patient substitutes the therapist for friends or family:

For patients with few social supports such as friends, family or work, the therapist may be positioned as a substitute for these supports. Boundaries should be appropriately discussed.

The patient sees treatment as a defeat:

The patient should be congratulated for courage in seeking treatment.

The patient is sabotaging treatment:

The therapist must confront and limit the behavior and describe it as acting out difficulties the patient has with other relationships

The patient takes the blame for family or group problems:

Depressed patients often feel excessively guilty. The therapist may educate the patient about this vulnerability and facilitate a change in her role in the family.

The patient is late or misses appointments:
The therapist should call attention and make associations to the patient's feelings in a nonjudgmental manner. If it continues, precipitants should be discussed and framework revisited.
The patient is silent:
Silence may be discussed, but should not be prolonged
The patient changes or avoids subjects:
Indicate when the patient changes the subject and explore any association with difficult material.
The patient is excessively dependent:
The patient must be informed about the boundaries and limitation of the relationship.
The patient attempts suicide:
 Initially, the therapist must determine if the patient needs hospitalization. If it is not necessary, then suicidal feelings should be explored and safety assured. The patient may need to discontinue psychotherapy, begin medication or consider hospitalization. The therapist must be very accessible during this period of crisis.
The significant other is asked to participate:
Conjoint therapy might be used to obtain 1) further information, 2) the cooperation of the significant other and 3) to facilitate improved communication.
The patient wishes to terminate early:
If the patient wishes to terminate, she should be asked if she is believes that her problems have been resolved termination should be explored. Remind the patient that she may return.
The patient has problems with self-disclosure:
The patient must establish trust in the therapist before she can be comfortable with disclosure.

DISCUSSION

Clinical trials have demonstrated the efficacy of IPT for the treatment of depression in many populations. I have described several clinical trials to demonstrate its efficacy in the perinatal population. My initial adaptation of IPT for perinatal depression (IPT-P) was at a time when perinatal psychiatrists were not yet using medications to treat depression during pregnancy. Today some women still choose not to take medication. This manual provides treatment guidelines for women with perinatal major depression who prefer not to use medication during pregnancy or lactation. It therefore provides a solution to the clinical dilemma of treating pregnant and postpartum depressed women with mild or moderate depression.

Nevertheless, I emphasize the necessity of proper evaluation to discern if major depression is mild, moderate or severe. Clinical guidelines from the American Psychiatric Association and the American College of Obstetrics and Gynecology suggest use of IPT-P in mild or moderate depression. IPT-P may not effectively treat severe depression leaving the woman with symptoms, prolonging her suffering and exposing her fetus and infant to the adverse effects of the mother's illness. Such effects include problems with behavior, cognition and creativity that often persist into early childhood and adulthood. Treating maternal depression provides prevention for children who are at risk.

This adaptation of IPT to the perinatal population is an adaptation of Klerman and Weissman's original IPT manual, which I highly recommend. As clinicians we owe a debt of gratitude to the work of Drs. Myrna Weissman and Gerald Klerman for their innovative work and dedication to the field of psychotherapy.

REFERENCES

1. Gavin NI, Gaynes BN, Lohr KN et al. Perinatal depression: a systematic review of prevalenceand incidence. *Obstet Gynecol* 2005;106:1071–83.

2. Gaynes BN, Gavin N, Meltzer-Brody S et al. Perinatal depression: prevalence, screening accuracy, and screening outcomes. Evid Rep Technol Assess (Summ). 2005;(119): 1–8.

3. Séguin L, Potvin L, St-Denis M et al. Chronic stressors, social support, and depression during pregnancy. Obstet Gynecol. 1995; 85 (4):583–589.

4. Hobfoll SE, Ritter C, Lavin J et al. Depression prevalence and incidence among inner-city pregnant and postpartum women. J Consult Clin Psychol 1995; 63(3): 445–453.

5. Frank E, Kupfer D, Jacob M et al. Pregnancy-related affective episodes among women with recurrent depression. Am J Psychiatry 1987; 144:288-292.

6. Wisner KL, Stowe ZN. Psychobiology of postpartum mood disorders. Brain, Behavior and Reproductive Function 1997; 15:77-90.

7. Graff LA, Dyck DG, Schallow JR. Predicting postpartum depressive symptoms and structural modeling analysis. Percept Mot Skills 1991; 73:1137-1138.

8. Farber EW, Herbert SE, Reviere SL. Childhood abuse and suicidality in obstetrics patients in a hospital-based urban prenatal clinic. Gen Hosp Psychiatry 1996; 18:56-60.

9. Dimitrovsky L, Perez-Hishberg M, Itskowitz R. Depression during and following pregnancy: quality of family relationships. J Psychol 1986; 12:213-218.

10. Zuckerman B, Bauchner H, Parker S et al. Maternal depressive symptoms during pregnancy, and newborn irritability. Developmental and Behavioral Pediatrics 1990; 114: 190-194.

11. Davalos DB, Yadon CA, Tregellas HC. Untreated prenatal maternal depression and the potential risks to offspring: a review. Arch Womens Ment Health 2012;15: 1–14.

12. Chung TK, Lau TK, Yip AS et al. Antepartum depressive symptomatology is associated with adverse obstetric and neonatal outcomes. Psychosom Med 2001; 63: 830–34.

13. Gressier F, Guillard V, Cazas O et al. Risk factors for suicide attempt in pregnancy and the post-partum period in women with serious mental illnesses. J Psychiatr Res. 2017; 84:284-291.

14. Preti A, Cardascia L, Zen T et al. Obstetric complications in patients with depression—a population-based case-control study. J Affect Disord 2000; 61: 101–06.

15. Steer RA, Scholl T, Hediger ML et al. Self-reported depression and negative pregnancy outcomes. J Clin Epidemiol 1992; 45: 1093–99.

16. Larsson C, Sydsjö G, Josefsson A. Health, sociodemographic data, and pregnancy outcome in women with antepartum depressive symptoms. Obstet Gynecol 2004; 104: 459–66.

17. Stein A, Pearson RM, Goodman SH et al. Effects of perinatal mental disorders on the fetus and child. Lancet 2014; 384: 1800–19.

18. Kurki T, Hiilesmaa V, Raitasalo R et al. Depression and anxiety in early pregnancy and risk for preeclampsia. Obstet Gynecol 2000, 95: 487–90.

19. Najman JM, Andersen MJ, Bor W et al. Postnatal depression-myth and reality: maternal depression before and after the birth of a child. Soc Psychiatry Psychiatr Epidemiol 2000; 35: 19–27.

20. Gelaye B, Rondon MB, Araya R et al. Maternal depression 1: Epidemiology of maternal depression, risk factors, and child outcomes in low-income and middle-income countries. Lancet Psychiatry 2016; Oct;3(10):973-982.

21. Wadhwa PD, Sandman CA, Porto M et al. The association between prenatal stress and infant birth weight and gestational age at birth: a prospective investigation. Am J Obstet Gynecol 1993; 169:858-865.

22. Dawson G, Klinger LG, Panagiotides H et al. Frontal lobe activity and affective behavior of infants of mothers with depressive symptoms. Child Dev 1992; 63:725-737.

23. Qiu A, Anh TT, Li Y et al. Prenatal maternal depression alters amygdala functional connectivity in 6-month-old infants. Transl Psychiatry 2015; 17;5: e508. doi: 10.1038/tp.2015.3.

24. Cerulli C, Talbot NL, Tang W et al. Co-occurring intimate partner violence and mental health diagnosis in perinatal women. J Womens Health (Larchmt) 2011;20(12):1797-803.

25. Palladino CL, Singh V, Campbell J et al. Homicide and suicide during the perinatal period. Obstet Gynecol 2011; 118:1056–1063.

26. Spinelli M, Interpersonal psychotherapy for depressed antepartum women: a pilot study. Am J Psychiatry. 1997 Jul;154 (7):1028-30.

27. Smith-Nielsen J, Tharner A, Krogh MT et al. Effects of maternal postpartum depression in a well-resourced sample: Early concurre t and long-term effects on infant cognitive, language, and motor development. Scand J Psychol. 2016 Dec;57(6):571-583.

28. Murray L. The impact of postnatal depression on infant development. J Child Psychol Psych 1992; 35(3): 343-361.

29. O'Connor E, Rossom RC, Henninger M, et al. Primary care screening for and treatment of depression in pregnant and postpartum women: evidence report and systematic review for the US Preventive Services Task Force. JAMA 2016;315(4):388–406.

30. Yonkers KA, Wisner KL, Stewart DE, et al. The management of depression during pregnancy: a report from the American Psychiatric Association and the American College of Obstetricians and Gynecologists. Gen Hosp Psychiatry 2009; 31(5):403–

413.

31. Wisner K, Zarin DA, Holmboe ES et al. Risk-benefit decision making for treatment of depression during pregnancy. Am J Psychiatry 2000; 157:1933-1940.

32. Klerman GL, Weissman MM, Rounsaville BH et al: Interpersonal Psychotherapy of Depression. New York, Basic Books, 1984.

33. Sullivan HS: The Interpersonal Theory of Psychiatry. New York, Norton Press, 1953.

34. Meyer A: Psychobiology: a Science of Man. Springfield, Ill, Charles C. Thomas, 1957.

35. Elkin I, Shea MT, Watkins JT et al. NIMH Treatment of Depression Collaborative Research Program: General effectiveness of treatments. Arch Gen Psychiatry 1989; 46:971-982

36. Spinelli MG. Endicott J. A Randomized Controlled Clinical Treatment Trial of Interpersonal Psychotherapy for Antepartum Depression. Am J Psychiatry 2003; 160:555-5

37. Mufson L, Weissman MM, Moreau D et al. Efficacy of Interpersonal psychotherapy for depressed adolescents. Arch Gen Psychiatry 1999; 56:573-579.

38. Weissman MM, Prusoff BA, Dimascio A et al. The efficacy of drugs and psychotherapy in the treatment of acute depressive episodes. Am J Psychiatry 1979; 136(4B): 555-558.

39. Brody AL, Saxena, S, Stoessel P et al. Regional brain metabolic changes in patients with major depression treated with either paroxetine or interpersonal therapy. Arch Gen Psychiatry 2001; 58:641-648.

40. Cuijpers P, Donker T, Weissman MM et al. Interpersonal Psychotherapy for Mental Health Problems: A Comprehensive Meta-Analysis. Am J Psychiatry 2016;173(7):680-7.

41. O'Hara MW, Stuart S, Gorman LL, Wenzel A. Efficacy of interpersonal psychotherapy for postpartum depression. Arch Gen Psychiatry. 2000 Nov;57(11):1039-45.

42. Spinelli M Endicott J, Goetz R. A Controlled Clinical Treatment Trial of Interpersonal Psychotherapy for Depressed Pregnant Women at 3 NYC Sites. *Journal of Clinical Psychiatry* 2013; 74(4): 393-399.

43. Spinelli M, Endicott J, Goetz R. Interpersonal Psychotherapy for Depressed Pregnant Women: A Reanalysis of Baseline Depression Severity. J Clin Psychiatry 2016;77 (4):535-40..

44. Klier CM, Muzik M, Rosenblum KL et al. Interpersonal psychotherapy adapted for the group setting in the treatment of postpartum depression. J Psychother Pract Res. 2001; 10(2):124-31.

45. Zlotnick C, Miller IW, Pearlstein T et al. Am J Psychiatry. 2006 Aug;163(8):1443

46. Brandon AR[1], Ceccotti N, Hynan LS et al Proof of concept: Partner-Assisted Interpersonal Psychotherapy for perinatal depression. Arch of Women's Mental Health 2012; 15(6):469-80

47. Grote N, Schwartz H, Geibel SL et al. A randomized controlled trial of culturally relevant, brief interpersonal psychotherapy for perinatal depression. Psychiatr Serv. 2009;60(3):313-21.

48. Grote NK, Katon WJ, Russo JE et al. Collaborative Care for Perinatal Depression Among Socioeconomically Disadvantaged Women: Adverse Neonatal Birth Events and Treatment Response. Depression Anxiety 2015; 32(11): 821-34.

49. Grote N. Katon WJ, Russo JE; A Randomized Trial of Collaborative Care for Perinatal Depression in Socioeconomically Disadvantaged Women: The Impact of Comorbid Posttraumatic Stress Disorder. J Clin Psychiatry 2016;77 (11):1527–1537.

50. Bhat A, Grote NK, Russo J et al. Collaborative Care for Perinatal Depression Among Socioeconomically Disadvantaged Women: Adverse Neonatal Birth Events and Treatment Response. Psychiatr Serv. 2017;68(1):17-24.

51. Lenze SN, Rodgers J, Luby J. A pilot, exploratory report on dyadic interpersonal psychotherapy for perinatal depression. Arch Womens Ment Health. 2015;18(3):485-91.

52. Miller L Gur M, et al. Interpersonal psychotherapy with pregnant adolescents: two pilot studies.J Child Psychol Psychiatry. 2008 Jul;49(7):733-42

53. Swartz HA, Cyranowski JM, Cheng Y et al. Brief Psychotherapy for Maternal Depression: Impact on Mothers and Children. Am Acad Child Adolesc Psychiatry. 2016 Jun;55(6):495-502.

54. Miniati M, Callari A, Calugi S et al. Interpersonal psychotherapy for postpartum depression: a systematic review. Arch Womens Ment Health. 2014;17(4):257-68.

55. Zajicek E in The experience of being pregnant. in Pregnancy: a psychological and Social Study Edited by Wolkind S and Zajicek E. London, Toronto, Sydney, Academic Press, 31-56

56. Benedek T. Parenthood as a developmental phase: a contribution to the libido theory. J Am Psychanal Assoc 1959; 7:389-576.

57. St. Andre M. Psychotherapy during pregnancy: opportunities and challenges. Am J Psychother 1993; 47(4): 372-590

58. Carr ML. Normal and medically complicated pregnancies in Psychological Aspects of Women's Health. Edted by Stewart DE, Stotland ND. Washington, London, American Psychiatric Press, 1993, pp.15-35.

59. Klein MH, Essex MJ. Pregnant or depressed? the effect of overlap between symptoms of depression and somatic complaints of pregnancy on rates of major depression in the second trimester. Depression 1994; 2:1994-1995.

60. Cox JL, Holden JM, Sagovsky R. Detection of postnatal depression: development of the 10-item Edinburgh Postnatal Depression Scale. Br J Psychiatry 1987;150(6):782–786.

61. Biringen Z, Robison J. Emotional availability in mother-child interaction: a reconceptualization for research. Am J Orthopsychiatry 1991; 61(2):258-71.

62. Cogill SR, Caplan HL, Heather A, et al: Impact of maternal postnatal depression on cognitive development of young children. Br Med J 1986; 292:116

63. Evans J, Melotti R, Heron J Murray L. The timing of maternal depressive symptoms and child cognitive development: a longitudinal study. J Child Psychol Psychiatry. 2012 Jun;53(6):632-40.

64. Scott D: Early identification of maternal depression as a strategy in the prevention of child abuse. Child Abuse Negl 1992; 16:345-58.

65. Weissman MM, Wickramaratne P, Pilowsky DJ et al. The effects on children of depressed mothers' remission and relapse over 9 months. Psychol Med. 2014 Oct;44(13):3211-2

66. Hamilton M: A rating scale for depression. J Neurol Neurosurg Psychiatry 1960; 23:56-62

67. Furukawa TA, Akechi T, Azuma H, et al. Evidence-based guidelines for interpretation of the Hamilton Rating Scale for Depression. J Clin Psychopharmacol 2007;27(5):531–534.

68. Thompson WM, Harris B, Lazarus J et al. A comparison of the performance of rating scales used in the diagnosis of postnatal depression. Acta Psychiatr Scand 1998;98(3):224–227.

69. Ji S, Long Q, Newport DJ et al. Validity of depression rating scales during pregnancy and the postpartum period: impact of trimester and parity. J Psychiatr Res 2011;45(2):213–219.

70. Rodríguez-Muñoz MF et al. PHQ-2 as First Screening Instrument of Prenatal Depression in Primary Health Care, [Spain] Rev Esp Salud Publica. 2017

71. Spinelli M, Endicott J, Goetz R. A Controlled Clinical Treatment Trial of Interpersonal Psychotherapy for Depressed Pregnant Women at 3 NYC Sites. Journal of Clinical Psychiatry 2013; 74(4): 393-399.

72. Spinelli M. Antidepressant treatment during pregnancy. Am J Psychiatry. 2012 Feb;169(2):121-4.

73. Calaway K, Coshal S, Jones K et al. A Systematic Review of the Safety of Electroconvulsive Therapy Use During the First Trimester of Pregnancy. J ECT. 2016

74. Kim DR, Epperson N, Paré E et al. .An open label pilot study of transcranial magnetic stimulation for pregnant women with major depressive disorder. J Womens Health (Larchmt) 2011; 20(2):255-61

75. Wirz-Justice A, Bader A, Frisch U et al. A randomized, double-blind, placebo-controlled study of light therapy for antepartum depression. J Clin Psychiatry 2011 Jul;72(7):986-93.

76. Keller MB, McCullough JP, Klein DN et al. A comparison of nefazodone, the cognitive behavioral-analysis system of psychotherapy, and their combination for the treatment of chronic depression. New England Journal of Medicine 2000; 342(20): 1462-1470.

77. Parsons T. Illness and the role of the physician: a sociological perspective. J Orthopsychiatry 1951: 452-460.

78. Raphael-Leff J. Psychotherapy and pregnancy. J Repro Inf Psychol 1990; 8:119-135.

79. Lewis E, Casement P. The inhibition of mourning by pregnancy: a case study. Psychoanal Psychother 1986; 2(1): 45-52

80. Lindenmann E. Symptomatology and management of acute grief. Am J Psych 1944; 101:141-148.

81. Lewis E. Inhibition of mourning by pregnancy: psychopathology and management. Br Med J 1979; 2:27-28.

82. Leon IG. Short-term psychotherapy for perinatal loss. Psychother 1987; 24(2):186-195.

83. Trad PV. On becoming a mother: in the throes of developmental transformation. Psychoanal Psychol 1990; 7(3):341-361.

84. Trad PV. Emergence and resolution of ambivalence in expectant mothers. Am J Psychother 1990; 44(4):577-589.

85. Brockington I, Cox-Roper A. The nosology of puerperal mental illness. Motherhood and Mental Illness edited by Kumar R and Brockington IF. Vol 2. 1988, pp 1-17

86. Robinson GE, Stewart DE. Postpartum Disorders in Psychological Aspects of Women's Health edited by Stewart DE, Stotland NL. Washington, London, American Psychiatric Press, 1993, pp 115-138.

87. Fonagy P, Sleed M, Baradon T. Randomized controlled trial of parent-infant psychotherapy for parents with mental health problems and young infants.Infant Ment Health J. 2016;37(2):97-114.

88. Miller LJ. Psychiatric disorders during pregnancy in Psychological Aspects of Women's Health Care edited by Stewart DE, Stotland NL. Washington, London, American Psychiatric Press. 1993, pp 55-70.

89. Iancu J: Psychiatric aspects of hyperemesis gravidarum. Psychother Psychosom 1994; 61:143-149.

90. Willson JR, Carrington ER, Ledger WJ. Obstetrics and gynecology, 7th Edition, St. Louis/Toronto/London, The CV Mosby Company, 1983.

91. Robinson GE, Wisner KL. Fetal Anomalies in Psychological Aspect of Women's Health Edited by Stewart DE, Stotland NL. Washington, London, American Psychiatric Press, 1993 pp. 37-55